ACQUIRED THROUGH

YO-DJM-825

ESEA Title IV B
Board of Education
City of Chicago

Marriage

Marriage

Jean Coryllel Lipke

Illustrated by Patricia Bateman

Published by
Lerner Publications Company
Minneapolis, Minnesota

The Library of Congress cataloged the
original printing of this title as follows:

Lipke, Jean Coryllel.
 Marriage. Illustrated by Patricia Bateman. Minneapolis,
Lerner Publications Co. [1971]

 61 p. col. illus. 23 cm. (A Being Together Book)

 SUMMARY: Discusses the important considerations of
marriage including housing, in-laws, sexual adjustment, and
children.

 1. Marriage—Juvenile literature. [1. Marriage] I. Bateman,
Patricia, illus. II. Title.

HQ734.L57   301.42′72′055   70-104896
ISBN 0-8225-0598-3   MARC
                                                  A C

52006

International Standard Book Number: 0-8225-0598-3
Library of Congress Catalog Card Number: 70-104896

Second Printing 1973

81-13857

✗Marriage is a partnership—a sharing. It is a sharing of experiences, thoughts, dreams, desires, fears, problems, work, responsibilities, and of all other aspects of living.

Growing up is basically a self-centered activity. Each person is concerned with his own progress and development. Everyone learns to make his own decisions and judgments, to know his own personality, abilities, and weaknesses. Once these and many other aspects of growing up are mastered, most people want to share their life with another human being of the opposite sex. As different as every individual is — in physical appearance, personality, intelligence, vocation, nationality, religion, financial situation — most people are alike in one way: they desire marriage. Statistics show that the majority of people do marry, at least once in their life.

✗ Yet marriage is often misunderstood ✗ For all of its popularity, there is probably no other condition that so many people enter for so long a time with so little understanding. The fairy tale ending of "they fell in love, were married, and lived happily ever after" is repeated so often from childhood on that people forget it is only a fairy tale. In the first place, men and women do not *fall* in love; they *grow* in love. Secondly, love is not the only basis for a successful marriage.* Finally, marriage does not guarantee happiness "ever after." Many starry-eyed young people would like to cling to this fairy tale, but divorce statistics are proof enough that a wedding does not automatically bring happiness. The increasing numbers of broken homes and hearts, and wasted years and lives, prove that people should find out more about marriage before they get into it.

Marriage *can* mean "living happily ever after." In fact, there is probably no other condition which can bring as much happiness to an individual as a successful marriage. If a man and woman know something about marriage, and if each is mature enough to really share himself with the other, their marriage has a good chance. This book discusses many of the areas of shared living which make up a marriage.

Another book in the Being Together series, Loving, gives information on choosing a mate.

ADJUSTMENTS

At first, marriage involves a lot of adjustments. It takes a while to make the change from living for one to living for two. Nothing magic happens during a wedding ceremony to change a single person into a married partner. Only time can do that. If two people have gone together for some time, then mentally they have been adjusting already. They are well acquainted with each other's personality, moods, temperament, and behavior in various situations.

In terms of this kind of adjustment, today's customs of going steady and engagement are far superior to an old-fashioned courtship. Years ago a boy and girl saw each other only on "dressed-up" dating occasions. Today a bride and bridegroom are usually aware of how their mate looks and acts in many circumstances. If they have dated many other people before choosing each other, they also have acquired some general wisdom about the opposite sex. Men know that women occasionally need to set their hair, wear face creams, and shave their legs. They know that there will be days when their wives will have little control over their emotions and perhaps be moody or weepy. Women know that at times men need to skip a shave, sleep in,

or grub around in the garage. Women also have learned that when days are tough at work, a man needs affection and comfort at home.

Even if two people know each other very well, there are always small surprises and adjustments. The sights, sounds, and smells of living closely with another human being take some getting used to, no matter how much in love a couple is. Hearing one's mate routinely brush his teeth and spit in the sink may be one adjustment. Finding dirty clothes anywhere but in the dirty-clothes hamper may be another. Modesty or lack of it sometimes takes time to adjust to. Single persons are usually not accustomed to being watched as they dress and undress. It might take time for a modest person to become used to seeing his mate go around with little or nothing on. A not-so-modest person might have difficulty understanding why his mate is uncomfortable at first. Procedures which are normal for one family and household are not necessarily normal for another. A newlywed unconsciously brings to his new home many of the patterns and routines from his former home. It takes a while for old patterns to become coordinated and new ones to be established.

RESPONSIBILITIES

Sharing responsibilities in a new home may seem too unromantic to consider, but if the work load is not balanced, it can cause great unhappiness. There are many variations on the basic work roles of husbands and wives, but newlyweds may profit from knowing the arrangements other couples have found satisfactory.

In traditional homes, wives are responsible for planning and preparation of meals, but husbands often share in shopping and clean-up. Some men are excellent cooks and enjoy preparing meals occasionally. Outdoor barbecuing has become almost exclusively a man's speciality. Wives are usually responsible for keeping the couple's clothes clean, pressed, and mended, either by doing it herself or having it done. Keeping the house or apartment clean is usually the wife's responsibility, although both partners share the task of keeping it picked up and neat. Calling a repairman when things break down is another job usually done by the wife. She makes sure that someone is home to let the repairman in and show him where the problem is.

Wives almost always take care of the entertaining that a couple does. The husband may decide to have his boss over or to give a small dinner party for the people in his department, or they both may decide that they want to spend an evening with a certain couple. The wife cleans up before and after the party, and plans and prepares the food. Thus she usually picks the date and extends the invitations. She does this, of course, after checking with her husband. Also, he checks with her when he receives an invitation, to be sure they do not already have something planned for that time. It avoids conflicts if just one person is in charge of the social calendar. A wife also has the responsibility of calling or writing a "thank you" to a hostess and host who have entertained the couple.

A husband's responsibilities have traditionally been more outside the home. He is responsible for earning money to support the couple, although many wives also work to supplement the husband's income. The husband usually takes care of the upkeep on the family car or

cars. He has more things to do if the couple lives in a house rather than an apartment. Lawns need cutting, watering, raking, and fertilizing, and in many parts of the country snow must be shoveled from walks and driveway. Often both partners share yard work, especially if they have gardens.

As times are changing and new ideas are being advanced, the traditional roles of husbands and wives are being redefined. Young couples, in particular, are breaking away from the stereotyped "husband" and "wife" roles of the past. Thus, while husbands are sharing or performing such "wifely" duties as cooking, cleaning, and washing, their wives are performing such "husbandly" duties as mowing the lawn, balancing the checkbook, and working outside the home.

Of course, the whole point is that any one of these tasks can be done equally well by either the wife or the husband. Each marriage partner may have done all of them during his or her single days, but if the couple shares the work load in marriage, neither person feels overworked or resentful. How the jobs are divided does

not really matter, just so both partners are satisfied that the work loads are fair. Sometimes newlyweds are so anxious to please their new mate that they will volunteer to do most of the jobs alone. This eventually leads to physical exhaustion, mental strain, and a feeling of resentment on the part of the person doing most of the work. It also leaves one partner very much out of the sharing that a healthy marriage needs. How long can a master love his slave or a slave his master? Marriage has to be a 50-50 deal, in which partners share the work as well as the fun.

There are other responsibilities to share besides work. Usually the husband is in charge of business and financial obligations. Both husband and wife should do the decision-making, but usually the husband takes the lead and makes the contacts. Such matters as buying insurance, applying for a loan or mortgage, paying major bills, engaging a lawyer — these are probably his responsibility. The wife often takes care of smaller financial obligations, such as grocery, laundry, and utility bills. Some women are better at budgeting than men; others simply can't keep track of money, and their husbands must do it for them.

The important thing is to share, whether the income is from one salary or two. If each person holds selfishly to his own earnings, just as when he was single, the marriage will suffer. Joint checking and savings accounts work for some couples. Others have one major account in reserve for large bills and use cash or another checking account for small bills.

Some men do not want to be bothered with household finances, so they just hand over their checks to their wives. They keep out a sum of money for their own personal spending and let their wives pay the bills and add to the savings from the rest of the salary. Other men prefer to keep their check. They take care of the financial obligations themselves and provide an allowance for their wives for personal and household expenses. Who controls the "purse strings" is not important, so long as both husband and wife are satisfied.

As in any partnership, it is unfair for either partner to use the finances for selfish purposes. The deciding factor for any major purchase should be, "Is it what *we* want?" instead of, "Is it what *I* want?" If the savings go for his new fishing gear or her new clothes, there may be resentment. Perhaps at the time each may rejoice in the happiness of his mate, but later on the purchase may become a source of irritation or jealousy. Small resentments and irritations can accumulate and build up into large-scale unhappiness or anger. By being fair with one another, especially in the use of family finances, a couple can prevent much trouble.

DEBT

The most common problem for newlyweds is debt. Once a couple has established some credit, large amounts of credit are relatively easy to get. Thus some couples get carried away when they set up housekeeping. They want new furniture, perhaps also a new car for the honeymoon, and they are eager to entertain their friends in their new home. Most young people want to have a home as attractive and convenient as they are used to or one even better. They forget how many years it has taken their parents to accumulate nice furnishings. In this day of "instant everything," many young people want "instant luxury."

Car and furniture salesmen, who offer long-term credit arrangements and low monthly payments, make instant luxury seem possible. New apartment buildings offer swimming pools, air conditioning, self-cleaning ovens, garbage disposals, dishwashers, and other conveniences to attract renters. But their rents are high. A car has become almost a necessity today, and if both husband and wife are working, they may each need a car. All of these expenses add up to quite a few monthly payments for several years.

Every month a couple has a rent or house payment, car payments, and heat, light, telephone, furniture, and appliance bills to be paid. Several times a year larger bills fall due, such as car and life insurance, income taxes, and for the homeowner, property taxes. Periodically a couple has medical and dental bills. There are weekly expenses for groceries, and daily expenses for lunch and parking if one or both partners are away from

home. Money is also needed for clothes and entertainment. Whether it is an evening at a good restaurant, or dinner at home for a few couples, one night of entertainment can double or triple the week's grocery bill. Vacations and trips must be planned for. To "fly now and pay later" is tempting, but in reality it may work a hardship on young marrieds. The week's pleasure may not be worth the months of paying.

As a young husband and wife begin sharing living expenses, they must decide which things are most important to them. If they have money enough for everything, there is no problem. If, as is most common, they do not, they have to decide where the money must go. For example, if they desperately want to join their friends for a weekend of skiing but find that the car insurance is due, they may have to give up or postpone their trip. On the other hand, rest and recreation are a necessity for many couples. Perhaps these couples could scrimp on groceries and entertaining for a few weeks and have enough money for both the car insurance payment and the ski trip. It all depends upon what is important to them. Most people put their money "where their hearts are." The money may be spent on immediate pleasures, or on savings and investments for the future. It may go for advanced schooling or a new car or boat. Where the money goes is not so important if the decision is satisfactory to both partners.

Problems arise when a saver marries a spender, a traveler marries a homebody, or an outdoor sports enthusiast marries a curl-up-by-the-fire book lover. Then how will their time and money be spent? These decisions are an important part of the sharing in marriage. The couple should agree; one person should not win his way and the other one lose. Marriage means compromising and understanding as well as loving.

MARRIAGE AND EDUCATION

Young persons who get married before they have finished their schooling face additional adjustments. Marriage is a sharing activity, but studying is a self-centered activity and cannot be shared very easily. Couples can share their study time together, but the actual learning must be accomplished by the individual himself. Some people go to school instead of having a job; others must work in addition to going to school. In either circumstance, married students do not have as much time together as other young marrieds. They have more time together, however, than if they were single.

The two biggest problems for married students are housekeeping and finances. Many single students live in dorms or at home and thus spend little time and energy on cooking and cleaning. When they are not in class they can be studying or earning money. A married student often has to be concerned with laundry, cleaning, cooking, and shopping, as well as studies and perhaps a job. If both husband and wife are in school, they will probably have to take turns with housekeeping duties, depending upon class loads and exam pressures. If only one of them is in school, the work load may fall totally on the other. Or if only one is in school the other may be working full time to support them both. A working wife or husband usually has free time for household duties or recreation. Thus one partner may in time feel bored or resentful because his mate must study during his free time instead of helping with the work or going out for some fun.

Another problem that arises when one person has to

work to help the other finish school is that the one in school may "outgrow" his working mate. The student's educational level rises, and his interests change; the working partner, who left school at a grade below his mate's, may not change in the same direction. If this happens, both of them have less in common, less to share, and less appreciation for one another.

The greatest difficulty that most married students face is expenses. Each has to pay for tuition, books, and fees for labs and special classes. In addition, married students have the usual living expenses all married couples have: housing, food, clothes, entertainment, insurance, car, transportation, and so on.

Married students usually have three ways to finance their education — loans, scholarships, and jobs. Many students borrow money for their education from the federal government or their school. This kind of loan has a very low interest rate and a long repayment period. Most schools provide scholarships, for all or part of the tuition fee, that are based on need as well as achievement. Many schools help students find jobs on or off campus if they need them. Some parents are willing to help their children finish school, by either loaning or giving them money for expenses.

Going to school while married requires a great deal of understanding and cooperation from both husband and wife and also their families, but it has worked successfully for many couples. Recent studies have shown that marriage often improves a student's grades. Perhaps it is because less time is spent chasing the opposite sex.

IN-LAWS

Consideration of parents is very important in a marriage. Young people may think that they are marrying just one person, but they are not — they are marrying a family. It is almost impossible to divorce a person from his parents, brothers, sisters, and grandparents. Consciously or unconsciously each marriage partner brings his family with him. This is especially noticeable at holiday time. Fortunate is the marriage where each partner accepts and welcomes the new family he has acquired through marriage. If a good relationship has been established before the wedding, so much the better. If not, the newlyweds would be wise to try to get to know, understand, and like their new in-laws as soon as possible. There may be some trace of resentment or jealousy to overcome; some parents feel that a "stranger" has taken their child away from them. However, if everyone understands that the new son-in-law or daughter-in-law is joining his mate's family, not taking a child away, the chances for good feelings with both sets of parents are better.

Another important point concerning in-law relations is that the newlyweds must stand on their own feet. Even though they are children of their parents, they are no longer dependent upon them, nor should they be controlled by them. Even if the young people had not achieved independence before, they must be independent after they are married. They must demonstrate that they are capable of the responsibilities of marriage — making their own decisions, supporting themselves, running a household, and paying their bills on time.

This is not to say that children should turn their backs on their parents once they are married. Their relationship is no longer one of dependence, but rather one of love and perhaps gratitude. In the excitement of a new marriage parents are sometimes forgotten and left out. Only when the newlyweds are parents themselves do they realize how much parents can miss their children. Occasional phone calls, cards, and letters help to maintain relationships and prevent unhappy parents on either side.

Many parents welcome their new son or daughter as the child they did not have. Her dad at last has a son to take fishing or hunting. His mom has a daughter with whom she can go shopping or share recipes. Both partners get an additional set of parents who love them and care about their future. Everyone can be the richer if relationships are begun with care, tact, and a sincere desire to be good friends. As in all aspects of a new marriage, it takes time to adjust to new relationships. It is more difficult for some to let go or change than others, and patience and understanding are needed from everyone. Occasionally personality differences make complete harmony and love impossible between a married couple and their in-laws. Mature young people, realizing that it is unlikely that they will be able to avoid one or both sets of parents forever, work to establish some kind of functioning relationship with their in-laws. Even if there is no love, there can be outward peace.

Once the young people start a family of their own, in-laws suddenly turn into Grandma and Grandpa, who are very special people to their grandchildren. It would not be fair to expect children to choose sides and like only one set of grandparents or aunts, uncles, and cousins. For these reasons especially, it is important that newlyweds make a special effort to win over their in-laws.

FRIENDS

A similar adjustment newlyweds have to make is accepting one another's friends. Probably they will like most of each other's friends, but not all of them. It is not fair for a new bride to expect her husband to give up the friends she does not like, and vice-versa. If, after several attempts, the new mate and the old friends absolutely cannot get along, it is probably best to see these friends separately. He could meet that "old army buddy" at his house for poker, and she could meet that "silly female" for lunch downtown.

If the disliked friend has an undesirable influence over one's mate, then a frank discussion of the friendship is needed. Sometimes a person can be so close to a situation or person that he can't really see the total picture any more. Perhaps the old friend needs to be re-evaluated through the eyes of one's new partner. If an understanding cannot be reached, then perhaps the friendship should be discontinued. It could be dissolved gradually so as not to hurt feelings. To maintain a happy marriage, one may have to put his mate's wishes over those of his friends.

Occasionally old friends are of the opposite sex, perhaps even old "steadies." Many people are able to maintain these friendships successfully after they are married. Others find that such friends bring problems. One's mate may feel jealousy, whether there is any cause for it or not. Or romantic feelings may develop unexpectedly and cause unhappiness. Here again, discontinuing some friendships may be the wisest choice.

81-13857

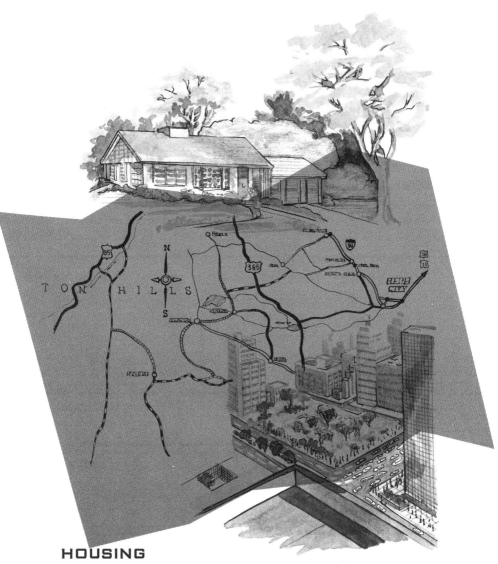

HOUSING

Choosing where to live is one of the first major decisions newlyweds make. If they settle too close to one or both sets of parents, it may create personality problems. If they live too far away, it may bring emotional and financial problems. Much depends upon the maturity of the newlyweds and the understanding of their parents.

Ideally a newly married couple should set up housekeeping some distance away from both sets of parents. A new husband and wife need a chance to be independent of their parents and dependent upon one another. The patterns and routines of their shared life must be established. They should be far enough away from parents so that they are not tempted to run to them if the going gets rough. This works both ways, too. Parents who are having trouble letting go may be tempted to drop in more often than they should if the young people live too close. Newlyweds need lots of time alone together to make the many adjustments that marriage calls for. Having too many people around slows down the adjustment process.

Living too far away from parents also may have disadvantages. To move many miles away to a new community, a new climate, and a new job or school may put additional strain on the marriage. The young people experience not only the usual adjustments of marriage, but also all kinds of adjustments to ordinary living. To "escape" from everyone and everything familiar may be exciting for a time, but once the newness wears off, loneliness may set in. A lot depends upon the maturity of the young people. If they have established an independent life for themselves before marriage, they usually are not bothered by distances.

Most newlyweds cannot afford to buy a house right away. Monthly payments on a house are often the same as rent for an apartment, but purchasing a house usually requires a large down payment. This down payment prevents many young people from buying a house as soon as they would like to. Also, buying a house usually means buying furniture and appliances. The minimum a couple needs is a stove, a refrigerator, and a bed, and these purchases create many expenses at one time. Thus a young couple may be better off to rent an apartment or a house.

Furniture may be a problem for young marrieds. Renting a furnished house or apartment is a solution for some. However, rent is 15 or 20 percent higher in furnished homes than in unfurnished ones. Many newlyweds borrow or buy used furniture from their friends and family. This gets them started and saves them money.

There are two reasons why a young couple might not want to invest a lot of money in furniture and appliances right away. The first reason is that good furniture is expensive. Cheap furniture may fall apart, sometimes before it is paid for, so it may not be worth it even as a temporary measure. Young people who buy a lot of nice furniture on credit may, after a few months, discover that they can't continue to make the payments. The furniture brings the strain of debt to their marriage. It becomes a great burden, a source of bickering and unhappiness.

The second reason not to buy a lot of furniture right away is that tastes and circumstances change. The Danish modern style that looked great in a new apartment may look out of place in the lovely old house a couple buys three years later. As young people mature, their ideas of what is attractive change. Major purchases should be put off until the couple is sure that the style they decide upon is not a passing fad or fancy.

They must also be sure that what they buy will be durable as well as lasting in appeal. Glass coffee tables, for example, may be fine in an apartment with two adults, but they may not survive in a house with children.

Many young couples enjoy furnishing their homes with "treasures" that they have purchased from used-furniture stores. They paint, mend, and polish these pieces to provide themselves with inexpensive, temporary furniture.

If finding a place to live seems financially difficult for newlyweds, perhaps one set of parents would let the couple move into their home for little or no rent. For many years it was an accepted practice for a young couple to live with one set of parents, usually the husband's. In many cultures in the world, this is still a widespread custom. In the United States today, however, this could cause all sorts of problems, and it might not be worth the saving. This arrangement has a greater

chance for success if the couple has had at least one year away from their parents. By then, most of the adjustments of marriage have been made, and the couple's shared living pattern is fairly secure.

Young people have the same problems when they live in a parental home that they do when they live too close to parents. Their independence is threatened, because both generations may slip back into their old roles of parent and child. Parents may consciously or unconsciously try to influence or control the activities of the young people. The son or daughter may begin to put the wishes of his parents before those of his mate. There may also be problems in the use of the kitchen or other rooms in the house. The work load and living expenses have to be divided fairly, so that one family does not become slave to the other. These are solvable problems, however. Much depends upon the maturity of the couple and the kind of relationship they have with their parents and in-laws.

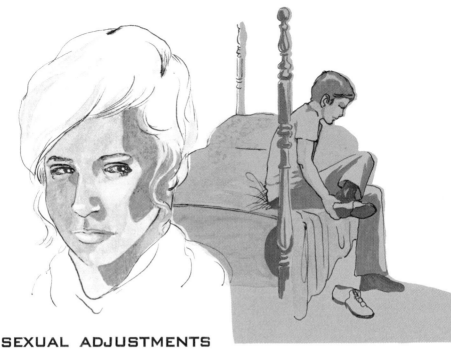

SEXUAL ADJUSTMENTS

The one adjustment unique to marriage and probably of most interest and concern to young marrieds is the sexual adjustment. Again, there are no magic words spoken at the wedding ceremony which will turn a person into a responsive, satisfying sexual partner. This, too, takes time, patience, and understanding. Each partner brings to the marriage different ideas about sex, conscious and unconscious feelings about sexual relations. Family background, religion, and education all have an effect on the attitudes one develops toward his body and toward sex. If a person has been controlling his sexual appetite for some years, it may be a while before he can relax and let himself enjoy sexual relations fully. Years of conditioning take time to undo. Perhaps a girl has been taught since childhood that sex was dirty or wrong, and she has been trained not to let anyone touch her. Then it may take time and understanding before she will respond to or enjoy her husband's touch.

Background is not the only influence on sexual adjustments. There are basic differences in the desires and responses between the sexes, as well as differences among individuals. Understanding and respecting these basic differences will help a couple establish a good sexual relationship.

Men are more easily and quickly aroused sexually than women. They are stimulated by sights, sounds, and odors more than women are. A man can be excited just by looking at a woman, not necessarily his wife, or by looking at pictures of women. A woman usually needs to feel affection for a man before he can excite her sexually.

Another difference between the sexes is that a man's sexual appetite develops at a younger age. One researcher claims that a man reaches his peak of sexual drive while he is still in his teen years. This same study indicates that a woman's sexual appetite is not fully developed until she is in her 30s. This difference may bring some amount of frustration to both partners. At the same time that a husband's sex drive is slowing down, his wife's sexual appetite is increasing. If they marry young, her desire probably will not match his at first; later, his may not match hers. This is one of many reasons why it is so important to understand the sex drive and how if affects each partner. Patience and understanding right from the beginning of marriage will help to establish a pattern for sexual relations that will satisfy both and will last.

It takes time to learn to use one's sex organs for

pleasure. Each must explore and experiment to find just what is most enjoyable for his mate. There are no rules, no right or wrong, no normal or abnormal sexual activities. The only standard for behavior is that it should be pleasurable for both. Sexual love is a sharing, and each person should share equally; one should not use the other for his own pleasure. As time goes on each will become more expert at pleasing his mate, and their sexual relationship will become more and more enjoyable. Many couples maintain a satisfying sex life well into their 60s and beyond.

There are several good marriage manuals available to explain to newlyweds some techniques of loving and sexual intercourse. There are also many outdated or sensational books available. It is wise to consult a doctor or someone else who is familiar with marriage manuals. Most doctors provide manuals on request and give them routinely to girls having a premarital physical examination. Such books are often rather technical, but they do provide information about the human body and how it can respond. If newlyweds add much love and tenderness to the advice in the manuals, they have a good chance of finding a satisfactory sexual adjustment.

Most sources agree that there are three stages to a satisfying sexual experience. The first is called *foreplay* or "love play." The second is the actual intercourse or *coitus*, and the third is called the post-intercourse or "afterglow" period. Each is equally important to the satisfaction of both partners.

Foreplay consists of any amount and combination of kissing, caressing, exploring, words of love — any expression of affection enjoyable to both. Foreplay can last minutes or hours. Foreplay arouses the body and prepares it for intercourse. When the husband is sexually aroused his penis becomes enlarged, erect, and hard. This is called an *erection*. It is caused by a rush of blood into the sponge-like tissue of the penis. A small amount of mucus usually is secreted from the tip, to act as a lubricant. When a woman is aroused blood flows into her sex organs, causing the tissue around the vaginal opening to swell. This tissue remains soft, however, and acts as a cushion or shock absorber. The *clitoris*, a small cylindrical organ above the vaginal opening, becomes larger and highly sensitive. The vagina secretes a mucus for lubrication. This makes it possible for the erect penis to slip into the vagina easily without causing pain. The inside walls of the vagina are very elastic and painlessly stretch to fit a penis of any size.

The second stage of sexual love is the actual intercourse. The husband inserts his penis into his wife's vagina. After a series of rhythmic movements they reach a peak of sexual excitement called a climax or *orgasm*. In a man orgasm is marked by the release of *semen* (sperm cells in fluid) in sudden spurts called an *ejaculation*. A woman usually feels a series of contractions within the vagina during orgasm. A husband and wife may not experience orgasm at the same time. If they do not, the husband may try to control himself until his wife has reached or almost reached orgasm. Then, because a man has more control over orgasm, he can perhaps time his climax to match hers. Coitus may take just a few minutes, and orgasm is over in a matter of seconds.

Following orgasm both husband and wife feel pleas-
antly exhausted. The release of sexual tension is followed
by an allover relaxation. It is important that they stay
in each other's arms following intercourse. Assurances of
love and affection are as necessary then as they were in
foreplay. Both may fall asleep, still in an embrace. Just
as it takes a woman longer to become sexually aroused,
it also takes her longer to "cool off." For women especially, then, the afterglow is a very real experience and
an important part of sexual love.

Every couple decides how often to have intercourse, what positions to use, and how much time to spend before reaching orgasm. Some couples have intercourse at least two or three times a week, others two or three times a month. Many couples use several positions for intercourse. Usually the couple lies facing each other. The man may be above the woman, the woman may be above the man, or they may lie on their sides.

A woman's first intercourse may be painful due to the tearing of a thin membrane which partially covers the opening to the vagina. This membrane is called the *hymen* or "maidenhead." It was once believed that if a bride did not experience pain and bleeding on her wedding night, she was not a *virgin*. (A virgin is someone, male or female, who has never had sexual intercourse.) Today it is known that strenuous exercise, the use of tampons, and many other causes can stretch or tear the hymen long before a girl reaches a marriageable age. Some girls have their doctor stretch the hymen before they marry.

One fact often neglected in marriage manuals is that both the lubricating mucus secreted during the arousal, and the semen, have an odor. The husband and wife should keep themselves very clean, especially their sex organs. Douching (rinsing the vagina) and deodorant suppositories may be necessary to keep a woman smelling sweet. Some cleaning agents are even medicated to help prevent vaginal infections. When two people live together so closely, each must take special care that their closeness is not spoiled by unpleasant body odors.

PARENTHOOD

Sexual intercourse is not only a source of pleasure, but it is also the way to parenthood. Most couples want to have children, although some do not want them right away. Children bring a special joy and fulfillment to marriage.

Raising a child is a very responsible job. To start a family is to commit oneself to at least 20 years of taking care of someone. In marriage one takes on the responsibility of caring for another, but at least that other person is an adult and capable of taking care of himself. This is not true of a baby. The human baby is probably the most helpless of all living creatures at birth. He is dependent upon his parents for many, many years.

Babies demand much time and attention. They must be fed, changed, and kept clean. They must be watched constantly so that they do not fall, cut themselves, or eat anything that might be harmful. Above all, they must be loved. Once a baby is part of the household, someone must care for him. He cannot take care of himself, so no matter how weary or bored or sick Mom and Dad are, they must answer the baby's cries or hire someone who will. Perhaps they long for a night out, just a chance to get away and maybe see a movie. But sometimes baby-sitters are too expensive or not available, or the baby is sick. It takes maturity to put aside one's own desires and do what needs to be done.

One must not become a slave to his children, however. Self-sacrifice cannot go on forever, nor is it healthy for parents. Mom and Dad must still be husband and wife to each other. Their new roles as parents must not cancel out their first roles as lovers and partners in life. It has been said that the greatest gift parents can give their children is love for each other. Children need to grow up in an atmosphere of love, secure in the knowledge that their parents love each other. Couples need time together alone, away from their children, even though it may take special planning and expense to arrange it.

Babies not only take time and attention, but they also are expensive. If the wife has been working and must quit her job, the couple has to learn to live on one income. A new wardrobe of maternity clothes must be purchased or made. The wife needs medical care throughout her pregnancy, and of course there are fees for delivery and her stay in the hospital. It would be wise for a couple to carry some sort of health insurance plan which has maternity benefits. Most companies require that the insurance begin at least 10 months before the baby is born.

A baby needs clothes, blankets, a crib, and diapers. If the wife does not have a washing machine available,

she may find disposable diapers or a diaper service necessary. There is almost no limit to the equipment one can buy for a baby — playpen, high chair, carriage, stroller, walker, jumper — nor is there a limit to the price one can pay for such items. Another expense a baby may bring is that of moving. Perhaps there is not enough room in the old apartment, or the apartment owners have a ruling against children. Moving itself is expensive, and a larger apartment or a house may also cost more money.

But babies are worth it. Creating a child can be called the ultimate sharing in marriage. The child shares

the heritage of both his parents and carries something of each of them into the future. And children are fun. They are worth all the work, expense, and self-denial they bring. Trying to explain the joys of parenthood to a nonparent is as difficult as describing the joys of marriage to a single person. It involves more feeling than reasoning, and it is almost impossible to share or understand someone else's feelings. Parenthood must be enjoyable, or people would stop having children. Today, because of modern methods of contraception (birth control), couples do not have to have children until they want to.

CONTRACEPTION

Children are such a responsibility, in both time and expense, that the decision to start a family is a very important one. Contraceptives make it possible for couples to plan their families. They also make it possible for a couple to enjoy sexual relations without fear of an unwanted pregnancy. There are several types of contraceptives available, some of which are more effective than others.

The most effective method of birth control is the oral contraceptive *pill*. This is a special hormone pill which the wife takes each day, usually for three weeks out of every month. Since some women experience unpleasant side effects from the pills, they must be prescribed by a doctor. The long-term effects of the pill, however, have not yet been determined.

Second to a pill in effectiveness is the *intra-uterine device* (*IUD*). An IUD is a small device, usually made of plastic, which is inserted into the uterus by a doctor. He removes it when the couple decides to have children. Many doctors give IUDs only to women who have already had a child.

The *diaphragm* and the *cervical cap*, two similar

articles, are the third most effective method of birth control. Both are cup-shaped devices that fit inside the vagina and cover the opening to the uterus. A doctor determines what size a woman needs, but she can insert and remove the device herself. The diaphragm is made of rubber and has a rubber-covered metal rim. It is inserted before a couple has intercourse and removed about eight hours later. It is used with a sperm-killing cream or jelly to insure its effectiveness. The cervical cap is usually made of plastic or metal, and it is smaller than a diaphragm. It is left in place for the three weeks between menstrual periods.

The fourth method of contraception is the *condom* or "rubber." It, too, is most effective when used with a sperm-killing cream or jelly. The condom is a rubber sheath that stretches to fit over the husband's erect penis before sexual intercourse.

The fifth method of birth control is the use of sperm-killing *chemicals*. These come in the form of creams, jellies, tablets (which dissolve inside the vagina), and foam. The foam is the most effective chemical, because it coats the walls of the vagina evenly and covers the opening to the uterus.

One of the least successful contraceptive methods is called *coitus interruptus* or *withdrawal*. The husband simply withdraws his penis from the vagina before ejaculation occurs. This is probably the oldest method of contraception known to man.

The least effective method of birth control is the *rhythm* method. This method is based on the fact that a woman is fertile for only one or two days a month. The couple avoids having intercourse around those days. The reason that this is not a very effective method of birth control is that it is difficult to determine the exact

days in which a woman is fertile. In fact, a woman's "fertile days" change from month to month.*

Each couple should, after consulting their doctor, experiment to find the birth control method that is most satisfactory. What works for some may not work for others. What is best at one time may not be best later on or after the couple has had children. More information on contraceptives may be obtained by writing to the Planned Parenthood Federation of America, 515 Madison Avenue, New York, New York.

*These contraceptive methods are explained in more detail in another book in this series, Conception and Contraception.

CONCLUSION

A successful marriage is like any worthwhile goal; it takes effort to bring it about. There are no magic words in a wedding ceremony, no magic events on a honeymoon. It takes time, patience, understanding, a willingness to share, and of course, love. Marriage is more than just sharing a name and address; it is a sharing of self.

For most people a day is divided in thirds. One-third of the day is usually spent in bed, another is spent at a job or school, and the other third is divided among a number of activities, such as meals, travel to and from work or school, housework, yardwork, and recreation. Marriage involves sharing as much of every day as possible.

The hours shared in bed receive the most publicity in magazines, movies, and television, and these hours are important to a successful marriage and the well-being of the marriage partners. However, some couples are happily married with little or no sex life, and others report having a satisfactory sex life right up to the time of their divorce. Thus the other two-thirds of the day are also important. If they are not shared happily, the marriage will not survive. The hours on the job or at school are not shared physically, but the earnings from jobs and the benefits of education are. Even when the partners are apart, each is working at home or outside the home to make a better life for them both.

One important way for a husband and wife to share the hours spent apart is to talk about them to one another. Conversation is extremely important for the success of a marriage. It makes it possible for each person to share his thoughts and the happenings of the day. Sad indeed is the marriage in which the husband comes home from work and reads the paper until dinner, relaxes in front of the TV for the evening, and then goes to bed without really talking with his wife. Such a man shuts his family out of his life even though he is spending time with them. Women at home all day especially need the stimulation of adult conversation. Equally disastrous to a marriage is the wife who is so wrapped up in the children or her career that she does not take time to talk with her husband. The exchange of ideas in conversation is a necessary part of a successful marriage.

Marriage means the creation of a new home, a new family, new traditions, and new routines. All these things represent a combination or coordination of two lives that now are shared. But marriage is still more than the sharing of traditions, wages, and hours in the day. It is a sharing of dreams and goals, and working toward them together; it is a sharing of fears and problems, and overcoming them together.

Two people choose to marry one another because they are in love, and each finds the other attractive physically, mentally, and spiritually. No one should expect that marriage will change his mate, or that he can change his mate into someone more desirable once they are married. Change can occur, but it comes from inside the individual. No outside influence, no mate or marriage, can force a change if the individual is not willing. The words "I do" are only the starting signal. Accepting, understanding, trusting, loving, forgiving, adjusting, and sharing — these are the words that lead to "and they lived happily ever after."

INDEX

ACKNOWLEDGMENTS

If the Being Together books give young people the answers they need to lead richer and more meaningful lives, much credit goes to those individuals who helped the author in every stage of preparing these books. Many gave freely of their time, knowledge, and experience, but my special thanks go to Robert W. Soll, M.D., Ph.D., *University of Minnesota Medical School;* Reverend Paul M. Youngdahl, *Associate Pastor, Mount Olivet Lutheran Church;* Reverend Thomas P. Hunstiger, *Pastor, St. Stephen's Catholic Church;* Adora Miller, R.N., *In-service Instructor, Fairview Hospital, Minneapolis, Minnesota;* Catherine Myers, R.N., *Head Nurse of Obstetrics, Gynecology and Family Planning, Outpatient Department, St. Paul-Ramsey Hospital and Medical Center, St. Paul, Minnesota;* James R. Bergquist, M.D., *Clinical Assistant Professor, Obstetrics and Gynecology, University of Minnesota Medical School;* Simon Davidson, *Family Counselor, Jewish Family and Children's Service, Minneapolis, Minnesota;* James Merrill, *Director of Child Welfare Division, Lutheran Social Service, Minneapolis, Minnesota;* and Barbara S. Teeter, Ph.D., *Lake Minnetonka Mental Health Center, Wayzata, Minnesota.*

JEAN CORYLLEL LIPKE

ABOUT THE AUTHOR

Jean Coryllel Lipke has spent most of her adult life working with young people. She has had many roles—educator, counselor, theatrical director, tutor, friend, and mother. A public school teacher in the Minneapolis-St. Paul area for nine years, Mrs. Lipke has taught English, remedial reading, theater, speech, and music. While working with young people and attempting to answer their questions, Mrs. Lipke discovered the need for honest, tasteful books dealing with human sexuality. After nearly three years of research, she began her work on this series.

Mrs. Lipke received her Bachelor of Science degree from the University of Minnesota's College of Education, with majors in speech and theater. A native of Minneapolis, she now lives in St. Paul with her husband and two children.

the being together books

PUBERTY AND ADOLESCENCE

CONCEPTION AND CONTRACEPTION

PREGNANCY

BIRTH

HEREDITY

DATING ☐

LOVING ☐

SEX OUTSIDE OF MARRIAGE ☐

MARRIAGE ☐

☐ recommended for junior and senior high only

We specialize in producing quality books for young people. For a complete list please write

 LERNER PUBLICATIONS COMPANY

241 First Avenue North, Minneapolis, Minnesota 55401